# START-UP
# RELIGION

# CELEBRATING HARVEST

## Ruth Nason

Evans

First published in this edition in 2011 by
Evans Brothers Limited
2A Portman Mansions
Chiltern Street
London W1U 6NR

Produced for Evans Brothers Limited by
White-Thomson Publishing Ltd,
2 St. Andrew's Place,
Lewes, East Sussex, BN7 1UP

Printed by New Era Printing Company Limited in Chai
Wan, Hong Kong, May 2011, Job Number CAG1637

Consultants: Jean Mead, Senior Lecturer in Religious
Education, School of Education, University of
Hertfordshire; Dr Anne Punter, Partnership Tutor,
School of Education, University of Hertfordshire.
Designer: Carole Binding

*Cover:* All photographs by Chris Fairclough

British Library Cataloguing in Publication Data
Nason, Ruth
    Celebrating harvest - (Start-up religion)
    1. Harvest festivals - Juvenile literature
    2. Fasts and feasts - Juvenile literature
    I. Title
    203.6

ISBN: 9780237543730

**Acknowledgements:**
Special thanks to the following for their help and
involvement in the preparation of this book: Sarah Crew,
Daniel and Nicole Rajan, and the children and staff of the
Grove Infant and Nursery School.

**Picture Acknowledgements:**
Art Directors/TRIP: page 16 (A. Tovy); Circa Photo
Library: pages 12 (John Fryer), 17 (Barrie Searle); Corbis
Images (Richard Hamilton Smith): page 7 (top); Exile
Images: page 21; Chris Fairclough Colour Library: pages
4 (right), 6, 7 (centre), 7 (bottom), 8, 9; World Religions
Photo Library: pages 18, 19.
All other photographs by Chris Fairclough.

# Contents

# Fruits and vegetables

Which of these fruits and vegetables can you name?

Do you know where they grow?

fruits        vegetables        grow

► **Do you sometimes eat satsumas?** •••••• **They grow on bushes or trees, in hot countries.**

**Which fruit or vegetable do you like best? How does it look and taste?**

shiny ✳ round ✳ smooth ✳ **rough**
crunchy ✳ **sweet** ✳ juicy

**satsumas**      **bushes**      **trees**      **5**

# Time to grow

Fruits, vegetables and other food plants take time to grow.

▼ Tiny green apples grow on apple trees in spring.

▼ In summer the apples grow bigger and ripen.

▲ At last they are ready to pick and eat.

.6.. plants apples spring summer ripen

► **This farmer is sowing wheat seeds.**

◄ First the seeds grow into green wheat.

► Then the wheat turns golden. It is ready to cut.

pick  farmer  sow  wheat  seeds  cut  **7**

# Harvesting

Picking apples and cutting wheat are two examples of harvesting. It means collecting the food that has grown.

▲ This farmer is harvesting his ripe wheat. The ears of wheat are used to make flour.

8    harvesting    collecting    ears    flour

◀ These people are harvesting coffee beans.

► Catching fish for people to eat is sometimes called harvesting the sea.

**How do you think farmers feel at harvest time?**

tired ✳ **worried** ✳ happy ✳ pleased ✳ **proud** ✳ thankful

coffee beans   catching   fish   sea   9

# Harvest thanks

Lots of food that grows is ready for harvesting at the end of summer. All the food collected is called the harvest.

Many people say "thank you" to God for the harvest. They believe that God made the world. They thank God for food and for everything that helps food to grow.

seeds

water

harvest   thank you   God   believe

How do all the things in these pictures help food to grow?

sun

farmers

soil

Thank you for

What would you say thank you for?

water   soil

# Harvest festival

Many Christians have a harvest festival at their church, to say "thank you" to God.

► They decorate the church. Can you see the bread which looks like wheat?

They say prayers and sing songs, to thank God for harvest.

Christians  festival  church  decorate

▶ Often children take food to the festival. It is **displayed** in the church.

▼ Afterwards, the food may be given to older people who live nearby.

▲ Look at the foods in these harvest boxes. Can you say which plants they come from?

bread   prayers   displayed

# Prepare for a festival

Perhaps you will have a harvest festival at your school. There can be lots to do, to get ready.

▼ What songs will you **practise**?

Cauliflowers fluffy ...

... and cabbages green

practise

▼ What **decorations** will you make?

finger painting

hand prints

collage

shaped bread

◀ Is there a story to act?

▶ What food will you give? What will happen to it afterwards?

decorations

# Sukkot

Jewish people have a harvest festival called Sukkot. It lasts for eight days in September or October.

People get ready for the festival by building a shelter called a sukkah. Every day of the festival, they eat their meals in the sukkah.

Jewish    Sukkot    shelter    sukkah

The sukkah helps people to think about a story from the Bible. The story tells how, long ago, the Jewish people lived in the desert. They made shelters like this.

God looked after the people in the desert and sent special bread, called manna, for them to eat.

Bible    desert    manna

# Inside a sukkah

Jewish people invite friends to eat with them in their sukkah.

◄ What have these people used to decorate their sukkah?

What do you think it would feel like to eat in the sukkah?

invite

Sukkot is a joyful time. People thank God for the harvest and for all the food in the world.

► There is a special way of saying "thank you". Each day, in the sukkah, someone waves four plants like •••••••••••• this. It shows the blessings of harvest spreading everywhere.

What do you do to show you are thankful for something?

joyful      blessings      thankful

# Wanting to share

▶ **Do you remember how Christian and Jewish people share food at harvest time?**

▶ **What do you share? Why do you think people like to share things?**

share

At harvest festivals, people think about all the food they enjoy. They also remember that, in some places, it is hard to grow food, and people are hungry.

► Many people give money to charities, which help people like this.

People who work for the charities take food to the hungry people. They also help farmers to grow more food.

enjoy          hungry          charities          **21**

# Further information for

**New words introduced in the text:**

| | | | | | spring |
|---|---|---|---|---|---|
| apples | church | enjoy | harvesting | prayers | sukkah |
| believe | coffee beans | farmer | hungry | ripen | Sukkot |
| Bible | collecting | festival | invite | satsumas | summer |
| blessings | cut | fish | Jewish | sea | thankful |
| bread | decorate | flour | joyful | seeds | thank you |
| bushes | decorations | fruits | manna | share | trees |
| catching | desert | God | pick | shelter | vegetables |
| charities | displayed | grow | plants | soil | water |
| Christians | ears | harvest | practise | sow | wheat |

## Background Information

Harvest is not part of the traditional church year, and may take place anytime in September/October. The first Christian harvest thanksgiving service is thought to have been in 1843, in an Anglican church in Cornwall, to encourage farmers to thank God for the harvest. Some communities have a tradition of harvest suppers. The Bible mentions thanking God for harvests (Psalm 65. 9-13), sharing the harvest with the needy (Leviticus 23. 22) and harvest festivals (Leviticus 23. 9, 16, 39-43).

The key concepts of harvest are thankfulness and sharing. The parable of the sower, often used at harvest festivals, is not really relevant to these. The story of the boy who shared his five loaves and two fishes (John 6. 5-13) is more appropriate.

If you are teaching about giving charity, it is important that the recipients' dignity is respected. Certainly paternalistic attitudes and racial stereotypes should be avoided. Many charities nowadays emphasise 'helping people to help themselves', such as the Christian Aid 'recycle a goat' scheme.

*Sukkot*, sometimes called the Festival of Tabernacles, is a Jewish festival to celebrate the gathering of the harvest, when temporary shelters were built near the harvest fields. It also commemorates the 40 years the Israelites spent in the wilderness, living in tents, having escaped from slavery in Egypt. The festival lasts for eight days. Today a temporary hut called a *sukkah* is put up for meals and socialising. Instead of a roof, the hut has branches decorated with fruit. This is to remember the time in the wilderness when the Israelites were protected only by God.

During the festival an important blessing takes place using four plant species, which today have special meanings: a palm branch symbolising the spine; willow branches symbolising the mouth; myrtle leaves symbolising the eyes; a special citrus fruit symbolising the heart. The four are held together and shaken during the prayers, to symbolise the involvement of the whole being in praising God. Prayers are said for the whole world.

On page 14, the harvest song that the children were practising is called "Paint-box" (words by V. P. Mitchell), from *Harlequin: 44 Songs Round the Year* (A. and C. Black). On page 15, the girl was acting out the story of *Handa's Surprise* by Eileen Browne (Walker Paperbacks).

# Parents and Teachers

## Suggested Activities

### PAGES 4-5
Ask children to identify fruits and vegetables from a shopping bag. Let them paint their favourite fruit or vegetable.
Place food labels/pictures around a world map, linking foods to countries of origin.
Make a dominoes or matching pairs game, with pictures and names of fruits and vegetables.

### PAGES 6-7
Draw out children's experience of growing and picking things.
Talk about seeds, watering, growing, blossoms, ripening, picking, and make sequence cartoons or zigzag books.
See how green tomatoes on a window ledge change colour as they ripen (mix paint colours to record this).

### PAGES 8-9
Read and let the children act the story of the Little Red Hen.
Learn a song, such as 'Thank you for the world so sweet'.

### PAGES 10-11
Children could conduct a controlled experiment growing cress seeds to show their need for water, warmth and light.
See how many languages the class can learn to say 'thank you' in. Make a harvest 'thank you' poster.

### PAGES 12-13
Visit a church with a harvest display, or watch a video of a harvest service.
Talk about what harvest gifts might be appreciated by people in the community.

### PAGES 14-15
Prepare for a school or class harvest festival. Make shaped bread, such as a mouse, wheatsheaf, or a platter shape with five loaves and two fishes on top. Tell the story from John 6.

## Recommended Websites

www.holidays.net/sukkot
http://www.somethingjewish.co.uk/uk_synagogues/
   (for list of synagogue contacts)
http://www.request.org.uk/infants/festivals/harvest/
   harvest00.htm (harvest photo on teachers' page)
http://www.christian-aid.org.uk/
http://www.cafod.org.uk/
http://www.tearfund.org/

### PAGES 16-17
Show a video of *Sukkot* or invite a Jewish visitor to tell about it.
Build a *sukkah* outside, decorate it with fruits and vegetables, and let children take turns to eat their refreshments in it. Tell the story from Exodus 16.

### PAGES 18-19
Let children invite guests to share food in their *sukkah*.
Talk about ways of showing thanks and gladness, such as thank you letters, grace before meals, applause, dance. Use the symbolism of the four species to show that gladness can be expressed by the whole being. Let the children make a card or a small gift for someone they would like to thank.

### PAGES 20-21
Talk about the joy of sharing with friends. Discuss an alternative ending to the Little Red Hen story, where they all share the bread. Which ending is happier?
Organise a sharing occasion, maybe making cream cheese and cress sandwiches, and other food incorporating fruits or salads.
Show sharing schemes from charities like Christian Aid, Tear Fund, CAFOD. Discuss thanking God by giving to others.

# Index